SandCastle

Rhyme Time

# Squeak from My Cheek

## Kelly Doudna

Consulting Editor, Diane Craig, M.A./Reading Specialist

ABDO
Publishing Company

Published by ABDO Publishing Company, 4940 Viking Drive, Edina, Minnesota 55435.

Printed in the United States.

Credits
Edited by: Pam Price
Curriculum Coordinator: Nancy Tuminelly
Cover and Interior Design and Production: Mighty Media
Photo Credits: BananaStock Ltd., Brand X Pictures, Comstock, Eyewire Images, Hemera, Image 100, Image Source, PhotoDisc, Stockbyte

Library of Congress Cataloging-in-Publication Data

Doudna, Kelly, 1963-
    Squeak from my cheek / Kelly Doudna.
        p. cm. -- (Rhyme time)
    Includes index.
    ISBN 1-59197-817-3 (hardcover)
    ISBN 1-59197-923-4 (paperback)
    1. English language--Rhyme--Juvenile literature. I. Title. II. Rhyme time (ABDO Publishing Company)

PE1517.D688 2004
428.1'3--dc22
                                                                    2004049107

SandCastle™ books are created by a professional team of educators, reading specialists, and content developers around five essential components that include phonemic awareness, phonics, vocabulary, text comprehension, and fluency. All books are written, reviewed, and leveled for guided reading, early intervention reading, and Accelerated Reader® programs and designed for use in shared, guided, and independent reading and writing activities to support a balanced approach to literacy instruction.

## Let Us Know

After reading the book, SandCastle would like you to tell us your stories about reading. What is your favorite page? Was there something hard that you needed help with? Share the ups and downs of learning to read. We want to hear from you! To get posted on the ABDO Publishing Company Web site, send us e-mail at:

**sandcastle@abdopub.com**

**SandCastle Level: Fluent**

Words that rhyme do not have to be spelled the same. These words rhyme with each other:

beak

speak

cheek

squeak

creek

unique

leak

weak

seek

week

During class, Alex rests her cheek on her hand.

Penny has a white bird with a black **beak**.

Gary's swing hangs from a tall tree near the **creek**.

Ford and his dad float on the pond in their raft.

They hope it won't **leak**.

When Barbara gets sick, she feels tired and **weak**.

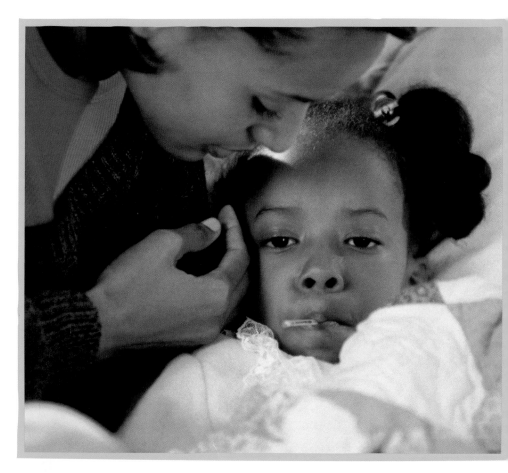

Harry's clown costume is not like any other.

It is **unique**.

Valerie covers her eyes and waits for her friends to hide.

It is her turn to **seek**.

Connor and Sharon **speak** quietly when they work in the library.

Jacob and Gina went to the beach for a **week**.

Elaine holds her guinea pig close to hear him **squeak**.

13

# Squeak from My Cheek

Perry the parrot's voice is weak.

He decides to seek help from Monique, who lives by the creek.

He opens his beak
to speak,
but all that comes out
is a little squeak.

Monique says,
"It's not too bleak.

I can teach you to speak,
just give me a week!"

Perry stays at the creek for a week.

Monique takes a look at his beak.

She says, "I know what to tweak.

Don't puff out your cheek, and don't let any air leak!"

Perry opens his beak
and begins to speak
in a voice that is strong, not weak.

He says, "This is unique!
Finally, there is no more squeak
from my cheek!"

# Rhyming Riddle

What do you call
an unusual mouth on a chicken?

Unique beak

# Glossary

**beak.** the hard, projecting jaws of a bird

**bleak.** hopeless

**creek.** a small, shallow stream that usually flows to a larger river

**tweak.** to make a small adjustment

**unique.** the only one of its kind; unusual

# About SandCastle™

A professional team of educators, reading specialists, and content developers created the SandCastle™ series to support young readers as they develop reading skills and strategies and increase their general knowledge. The SandCastle™ series has four levels that correspond to early literacy development in young children. The levels are provided to help teachers and parents select the appropriate books for young readers.

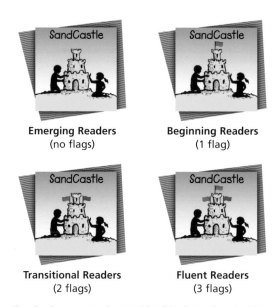

**Emerging Readers**
(no flags)

**Beginning Readers**
(1 flag)

**Transitional Readers**
(2 flags)

**Fluent Readers**
(3 flags)

These levels are meant only as a guide. All levels are subject to change.

To see a complete list of SandCastle™ books and other nonfiction titles from ABDO Publishing Company, visit www.abdopub.com or contact us at:
4940 Viking Drive, Edina, Minnesota 55435 • 1-800-800-1312 • fax: 1-952-831-1632